Within Firefly Fields

Elisa Reino

BookLeaf Publishing

India | USA | UK

Presentation by *BookLeaf Publishing*

Web: www.bookleafpub.com

E-mail: info@bookleafpub.com

ISBN: 9789357215275

First edition 2022

To the dragonfly soul who, always tethered to me, even through a journey of their own, returned to my life when I most needed it, guiding me gently back to myself. She said to me, one November evening, and it rings true every day of my life since then,

"If you lay still and quiet enough, you would see the sky fill with the glows of lighting bugs… dancing lights of joy…"

Let this collection be a humble gesture that proves the existence of one, hopeful, dancing light of joy within your firefly field.

ACKNOWLEDGEMENT

Gratefulness pours out of me - for those in my life that have seen me through, and stayed. Family that stretches beyond the realm of birth and blood. Family, of birth and blood, that shows me they exist, too, in love. I am most grateful for hummingbirds and dragonflies, the salt of the earth. For the professors and teachers who taught me how to read through the world. For Perspective - how lovely you are. For Patience - ever Life's teacher. Boundless gratefulness and humility, for this life I can call my own. It's been time to live, and so, magnificently, extraordinarily, I simply must.

May life always show you how to look for the beauty of its immense, still moments.

PREFACE

What is want. To want. Desire, appetite, necessity, yearning, envy, ache… This is a place where everything culminates, cultivates. I want to give what I know and feel, of my love, to those around me. There is so much of me to give. I want to give it, a little bit to each person I come into contact with. I want the genuine, I want the candor, I want the rawness that makes us human and connects us. That is what I want. I want to feel it in the chasms of me where I've thought no one must ever come into this place. Where I thought I'll never feel again. I want this to grow in me, perpetually, throughout every part of my being so that I am love. I want this feeling to stay, most of all.

What an extraordinary position to be in, as well, as someone who can want. To be able to say, yes, this does please the depths and gravity of my soul, give me more. Or, even, it has satisfied me, and I am deliciously contented; there is a peace within my soul. And yet, to say, no, lovely thing, no, this is not the want of me – how beautiful. Ever changing, ever dynamic, the growth of want, and the growth of its seasons.

Then, I want to write it. I want to relive every beautiful, divine moment. I want to feel the words pour out of me and create this tangible perception. Paradise is this life. I want it to be infectious. This absolute, carnal, depth of want. In each iteration of life that I am in, I want for this to be my perpetual want. With each death of these iterations, I want to be bathed in all of the ache, all of the wants, desires, envies, necessities, all of the love.

I want my children to know this both of me and for themselves. I want their lives to be drawn out in front of them, a perpetual sunrise, a perpetual yearning for the want to be felt, but of utmost importance, to feel. I want this to be how they mean "falling in love." My want to desperately fall into this chasm of love and never withdraw from it. I want to write it into eternity, what we know of it, anyway. For this to exist, always. For someone. I want this to be my legacy, this and this alone. I will have been fulfilled, then. My soul can find its rest.

Then, I think, perhaps, in these thoughts, I am not new to this world. I have been. I have existed. I can feel it in the origin and the heart of me. Perhaps, however, I am new to love - and so, my extraordinary fascination with it. This curiosity of the enchanting. The unknown. How quick we are to fear what is not known to us, and yet, there is nothing ever known to us. Everything we know, everything that we experience is novel in the moment. What is the grand ether of space? What is a galaxy but singular moments of life, of light, together. One light shining on another, and the next… Where time nor space are entities with grandeur – in this, these things, these moments, just are. They shine, they pulse, they exist. They are beautiful. They must feel. What if this is the whole and the cause of how and who we are, where we came from – this chasm of love, where the more it is given, the more it is felt, the more it is given back. At the core of love, in any form, is belonging. This is not a new sensation, or curiosity, or search. This is not a new want. It has existed ages before me and will continue to exist in the cosmos after me – it currently flows through me fiercely, ravenously, I must indulge in it, for it, with it, and because of it.

So, we come back to the intendment, what do I want for? To feel, to feel a boundless, unrestrained sense of every living emotion, to never lose it, for it to exist, always – the greatest of these, love.

Still, Life

    That this woman looks like
the rest of my life is not accidental—
curious and ardent like
the breath of today, a fiery furnace,
the sun seen from underwater,
flickers of golden streaks
dancing along, a vision
just out of reach.

    If only I could get a hold
of the whole of her, the way wind
envelops hair, the way a child grabs
his mother's finger, with the whole of his hand;
how a smoker lifting cigarettes in chains,
then bridges of ember, always breathes for last
breaths – a discipline, precisely pointless,
a moment here, then gone.

    To lie in a field, together, tracing the letters
of my name across her chest, letting every
thing listening know where my life was made;
we lay in that whispering grass, to forget what
we were,
and yet, to become more brightly human.

Our eyes find rest - the landing of a
dragonfly,
on our knee. A silent patience, a gentle
nod, then off again, it ventures effortlessly
into immensity.

Heartsong

Sitting next to you, close, leg crossed,
my knee lays gently over your lap, you rest
your hand there, effortlessly,
as if it were second nature. Nestled in,
there was a level of comfort known only
to lifelong couples; I sat still
to let this comfort consume me.

The light of the fire cast a golden tone
captured by your eyes – a delicious
caramel hue. I watched the flames reflected
on their surface; the desire to hold you close and
dance
along with the flames played out, a vision in this
reflection.

The warmth from the fire was
over-taken from the heat of our closeness;
the chill in the air was kept at bay.
Laughing, singing, listening, smiling…
just being. We lived
a lifetime in that moment.

Ocean Psalm

Your breath, hallowed water that dwells
in all things; I float on your words, a leaf tossed
in currents, moving from realm to realm –
Pale clefts of moon, drawing out decisions

on each ripple of ocean, each current
its own path; my soul knows
your current, only the moon directs me
to you in her own time.

She leads me where the cosmos bloom,
brings my soul so near to blossom; how
beautiful
when not always full, the ache to fill, a promise
given long ago, pray it with me.

Devoted Earth, resplendent Night,
Sea that offers and refrains,
Pines that cling to cliffside in awe, all breathe
the same old covenants

into the golden dawn:
Restore my place,
in the territory of things,
that belong to us.

The Tendency to Freckle

This poem comes to me
in between whispers and wants,
in the music of bird song,
en el susurro de las olas,
within piano melodies.

This house of hollow
I have built, grown
accustomed to these walls, how
they resound at the hum
of my bated breath;
solita.

I want so much to drown in you –
to sink deeper into your tide pools,
inundate myself with your scent, never
exhale. The taste of you drips
from tongue to chest, a slow
haste, warm honey.

Your release, from a depth
that is hard to come
out from – tide pools full,
fill me with both reverence,
restraint.

A yearning, a quiver-sigh from so profound,
I am certain there is nothing left of me,
only to grasp life at your surface again;
I pull myself up by your thighs, there is not
much left of me:
an urgency to breathe you in.

There's sun at your destination. Yes,
it's you – warm me, become me,
become you, become eternity –

It feels like the sun, reaching for you,
clouds unveiling, bare skin,
strength of warmth radiating.

How long the Sun has lived, and yet,
never said, You owe me;
look what happens with a love like that,
one can be loved into being.

Ode to Your Hands

I. The Canyon Period

Your hands curl, tendrils wrapping
and grasping at forming thoughts,
feelings; sensations of static
sounds of an ocean of cellos,
fermata in tawny hue.

Within your palm, triad of peaks and valleys,
intentional cleft, chasm of deliberate and careful;
in the movement of conversation, your touch
softens.

The canyon is not unlike your hands – space
between
fingers – what can be held and what falls –
Gravity pulls from within: fruit, leaves, stars,
planets,
hearts; fall like autumnal valleys,
surging with currented winds.

Your canyon, I found, without compass,
which, unnecessary when you search for fervor;
carved through in time, resounding hollow,
stripped of and from yourself.

When the crests and troughs of me, find
the peaks and valleys of you, rigid
transformation
reflects in perfect form; the horizon evanesces,
leaving
only the frequency of vastness - the solitude of
knowing it.

The quiet fluttering of steady, swift wings,
flash of iridescence whirs by;
the lone Psalm's monophony echoes:
How long have you existed, here?

II. The Juniper Period

Knurled, unfurled, there is an arching, an agony
–
this twisted contortionist finding life, says
Fuck you, Drought. I will
survive you; I will laugh and it will be
magnificent
and I will be exquisite. I have come from the pits
of you, this earth, I have come, carved and
refined;
I have learned you, I do not allow you
to own any part of me.
In the strength it takes for the capacity to
survive,
here exists the Juniper tree; out of sheer refusal
to die, she sheds parts of herself –
the parts that can be let go – that can be offered
up willingly to Death -
She lets these pieces of herself go
without hesitation. She proclaims,
Something has tried to kill me, and it has
deliciously failed,
celebrate me; the endurance of my flesh and my
blood.
Then, rapture occurs –
unfolding, opening, rebirth, growth;

in the patience from survival to life,
Divine transformation. Life, at the fingertips
of the Juniper, soul-spring oasis, chirping,
splashing, buzzing –
The Earth pulses with intensity; the flutter
returns, sunrise reflected in lustrous mosaic
of blue-greens, scarlet-golds, opalescent
yellows,
caught in suspension, resting at the tip of Life,
facing the vastness of the canyon;
life below, life above, within, outstretched,
reaching outwards, upwards, ever expanding –
The dragonfly takes flight, suspended in
animation,
emerald eyes gazing, wishing
the Juniper farewell,
Te veré de nuevo.

III. The Amplitude of the Poet

When something transcends,
through planes of exist-
ence, trace gravity;
within the pull, find

love does not conclude,
it accumulates,
swells - grows - expands in-
to eternity.

The dragonfly, poised,
pioneer, pausing…
finding the essence
of life takes time,

Be patient, wild heart.

These are not branches
of sorrow, no, they are
branches of humble
defiance – find the

movement, captured in
time, the still transfer

of energy from
one medium to

another – the earth,
the canyon, the tree,
me. I am the still-
ness, the movement, I

am this tree, nodding,
grasping, reaching for
the immensity;
saying, loudly, in-
to this world, feel me;

I am with you.

On Devotion

Small tendrils of gold spun silver curl their way
around my fingertips; the warmth of cheek
on thigh and smell of apricot teases me
enough so I recite what I know of prayer:

My God, I am in Heaven –
sacred is my name on your tongue,
Come, you beckon,
let me do to you as you've done
to me, here, in this bed,
to keep you;

Allow me to give you everything
you need, blame me
for all broken promises, and forgive
those who've broken us on whims.
Lead me not towards the forgotten,
but deliver me, again and
again, into eternity.
Amen.

Dalliance

Let me fill this page with black lace and you,
undo me, make me again,
teach me how to be had, listen
to me let go; curious finger
tips, exploratory kisses, swirl of tongues,
wandering mouthfuls of you, I drip.
My lips seek stories of pleasure, Honey,
hold my gaze, I want
to read you.

There are many kinds of open –
how a mouth forms a sound,
forms a word, forms your name;
within the pages of me, splayed
at the spine, broken yet fuller now;
ache that leaves the door unlocked,
windows open, letting the oceans of light in.

One day, I could open
you in full blossom, caress
your spine as one does
with new books; slow tenderness,
nervous energy pulsing, whispers of turning
pages, nape of neck, the want
to be gentle, the fervor of reaching

your climax; you've ebbed and flowed
through my life, waxed and waned,
so I have only ever caught glimpses of you.

Pale moon seduces in phases; let me learn
your desires, so look at me, in me, lace
your hands through my hair, pull me higher,
let me feel your staccato pulse and place
galaxies
on the crescent of your neck, collarbone valley,
kiss every freckle of you, every in between, my
breath
on your breasts, my breasts tracing your navel,
push
me, place me, put me where you need me, press
yourself into these sheets, my hands, your hips,
my tongue, your lips, sweating silhouettes,
canyons that curve.

Skin stuck to humid skin, hold me steady
by your thighs; I find my course as you sail in
me, find
my secrets, undiscovered, uncharted flesh
into blossom, unfurl in me the treasure, unclasp
the gold
still hot from my body, spill me selfishly, cradle
me
on your tongue; ravenously, I want to swallow
the nectar of you, elixir of ecstasy, Honey, slow

dripping of eager breaths;

I want to discover the pearl
you are forming, take you into the depths
of me, rose-wet cavern, current of desire pull
and pulls through me, I pause over you, the
waves
coming over the sand, I, coming over you,
My body writes into your skin the poem you
make
of me, fill me until I overflow;

I am desperate for you, to pleasure, I surrender,
take me, where the whole of me is, pulsing
with every anticipated touch; touch my soul
again and again, deeper, slower, quench
my drought with your eager wetness, cover me
in you, in this, in no time before or after;
preserve us in this pleasure purgatory,
where I cease to exist as I, where we begin
to meld into one, where it is your eyes that close
when mine roll back, it is your moan I hear
when my mouth opens for you.

Waning

your voice echoes
through my walls
our rhythm carving
into time
what love sounds like
our bodies are places
of worship
the swelling of our climax
our hips rocking together
rhythm of prayer
coming together
the beating of your heart
that sounds like mine
the moment after
intensity
sounds like
my breath
returning to me
I am weak
in the stillness of my studio
stillness that returns me
quiet tide that runs
courses through, then
out like ripples
breath from within

absolute essence of me
breath of satisfaction yet
still, the want
to lay with you unwound
with what remains and
the rest, in this end
together

Celestial Skeletons

The universe exists as one energy,
transparent weight, gravity that ascends,
I am convinced, there are three
realms of existence: the Divine,
Nature, and Humanity; where Humanity
is the last plane, sunken – some who exist
here, can transcend into the other
realms, found moments of Divinity, carried
in whole emotions, seemingly lifted,
palms upwards, for brief moments,
one can dwell in the divineness of Nature,
of the spiritual, even;
superficiality, the chains
that can keep us tied
in only one plane. In the same moment –
in which you reached
across the space between us,
spanning through the time amidst
us, extending to touch, bringing me
closer to you, planting a kiss in the middle
of words – the tether of us abridged;
the beginning and the end, the ancient
of days, the great Love, transcended
through all realms and kissed me, right
on my lips.

The Bounding Main

The flowing river that leads us
to the ocean – where
do my waters end and yours begin?
I have never felt the vast
quietude in my soul that Buddhist monks
seem to spend their entire lives
attaining, and so, because I am no Buddhist,
or monk, on the quest for inner peace, I know
nothing
of what this means,
what I do know, I feel,
and I feel that this day, with you, is
as close to the feeling of tranquility
I have ever known. All within me, lulled
into rest, the tumultuous winds that disquiet
me, resolved; clarity of water, of mind,
warmth of love, closeness; you showed me
what was yours, held me in the middle
of this place where life bustles around
us, something rustles in the bushes behind,
there are so many birdsongs – wind through
the trees like the earth exhaling,
crossing the threshold of the door,
leaving muddied boots just outside,
Home, this place, with you;

in this home, there is a porch swing
where we'll sit, you, with your books
and tea, steeping, I, with my journal,
cafecito a mi lado, steaming, entanglement
of limbs and blanket; you're reading
but not really reading, I see you,
I'm writing and not really writing, either,
I kiss the back of your hand,
your fingers, your palm, pressed
to my cheek so you can feel
me smiling.

Flor de Oración

What does a flower give?
As long as we'll have them,
they'll continue to give of themselves,
freely, never demanding,
giving boundless life.
Each bloom, a soul
blossoming, existing,
independent of us, and yet
dependent of unpredictability
to show resilience, strength,
determined to live a life of beauty.
Those that are summoned,
by the flowers, find
nourishment for their life, find
a home, a resting place, renewal.
Flowers beckon those that provide
pleasure, in turn, this flower will make
new life from this meeting.
Any creature, exploring,
leaves with its essence,
to spread it, to make new
life elsewhere. Oh,
the ritual of giving,
intimate connections,
it is easy to think this flower

God, and why couldn't it be?
Swaying, in the breeze, lilting,
dulcet whispers; I find myself
on my knees, hands both grasping
soil and bearing my weight –
Mercy.

Here, we are

by the fire; talking on what is meaning,
what is purpose. We sing, wonderfully,
enjoying the playlist the bar chose
for the night. We laugh into the current
of the fire; it radiates toward us,
warmth reaching through the cool wind;
in the same way, I am drawn to you.

We sit together, the excitement of
skin touching skin; your smile, lingering
in the corner of my eye; I feel the gravity
of you. I see our lives, in the heat of the flame,
these visions, dancing around us;
melodic mirage carrying us into the years ahead:

The birdsong sneaks in through open windows,
the sun streams unto us; a sigh over takes me,
a stretch, a yawn; my eyes find the courage to
open,
Ah, There you are… kiss me.

Here we are, in this world,
in this home, in this bed,
within each other's arms,
in love, still.

Heartwish

Bantling Sun, warming,
birdsong exclamations,
sound of stillness, flecks of earth
floating gold, suspended in light;

From the bedroom, I walk
to find myself in a room, full
of those that I find belonging –
mami, papá, hermana, hermanos, esposa mía
futura.

I do not walk alone, She follows me:
small, brown, long-haired umbra;
inky ringlets, her shadow, she giggles,
shrieks in delicious delight of fullness.

Barefoot, I sit on the floor, prop myself
against the nearest couch. Little Life, You,
full of laughter, happy squeals; I cup-pat
your tender back, a sound of deep hollow –

Hollow of my hollow, laughter of mine,
you breathe for life between these squeals,
joyful utterances, gasp of breath, and again,
calling out in joy; you stand, now, on the couch,

tottering on mercurial cushions, your hands find
my hands, your weight falls into my gravity,
gracefully;
the world around us, looks on, in, I, too, feel
their emanating rapture, but I, enraptured

only in you, your enamouring coos, find yourself
in my lap, this asylum of limbs and breast,
I watch you watch me; my hand rests
on your tender diaphragm, breath of life,

rising and falling within you; your budding
hands rise to nestle my face, I lean into
your vernal palms, a swelling, a welling
of spring rain, eases from slope of cheek,

curve of lips, precipice of chin, transcends
the realm of space, settles, tenderly,
in the tan-paleness of your spirit. I see
everything in creation, in you, sweet, joyful
creature.

What is this source that is both
question and answer? Unspoken
desire, you exist without words,
you are, profound and vast.

The place we all retrace, innate

navigation of the how and the way,
archaic compass, heart of life;

Never not there, never will be not;
gateway without birth, nor death, only puzzle
of wordless being; certain in Death and Life,
recognition of essence when nothing else.

Enter the nowhere of immense
value: the melody of love songs, tender whispers
of lovers, the endless wants of desire, of
selflessness
defined to a finite lifetime – yet, an infallible
being

beyond space and time; depth of heart-cavern,
hollow of my hollow, sanctuary of boundless
love,
atoms that are my atoms that are your beautiful
atoms;
worthy, purposeful breath: heartwish being.

On being a Poet in Love

the way it feels to wake
at noon, grind the coffee, taste
silvery seduction, sit on the steps
of my studio, and write
about a thunderous afternoon;
to be so filled, finding everything
so extraordinarily beautiful.

Saeculum

woman who speaks
with the trees
trees that tell this woman
I have what you seek
each listens for the other
breaths that pause
lilt that provokes
the Healing World

women that walked this earth
among new woods
uncontested, lily white
woods that would speak
to these women
women who would listen
use my leaves, women
stay away from my flowers
women, take these roots
with you into your passions
into all women's endurance
retrace this compass infinitely

woman who returns
to her trees
trees that call out to you

mother that returns to her daughters
drawn to hold their hands
as she teaches them to retrace
the equinoctial colure

Heart's Song

Let this page give refuge
to your garden heart
ever growing, ever tended;
when there is sun, come to
this garden to see in
new light, when there is rain,
come to this garden, barefoot,
and weep, cultivate the ground
beneath you, find sure footing,
hold my hand, too,
take me with you, wherever
you go.

Years ago, you walked ahead
of me, delighting in these fields;
I watch you walk through streaks of sun,
running your hand gentle
across the flowers and tall grass,
my gaze is pulled behind us,
footprints that hold springs;
I come back to you,
you are unearthing a flower, detangling
roots, holding tender,, this fragile life –
you are talking, no, singing,
reminding it how beautiful it is.

The melody surrounds me,
it is within this garden,
in my heart, a soul-song,
You. Pequitas, my song is you.

Within Firefly Fields

& so we return,
barefoot, to this Holy Land,
prostrate, bared,
delightfully drained;

weight of the world, press
Atlas, endure – for me, for you;

promise
the rest of our lives,
yours to mine,
mine to ours,

I love you,
tremendously,
always;

siempre,
tanto,
te amo.